Making the Modern World
Nineteenth-century Britain

Keir Hardie
and the Labour Party

John Robottom

Longman

Keir Hardie

Miners' homes near Glasgow, drawn when Keir Hardie was 21

The home in which James Keir was born in August 1856 was a tumble-down thatched cottage in a village about eighteen miles from Glasgow. His mother, Mary Keir, was a servant. Three years after James was born, Mary Keir married David Hardie. With their son, now called James Keir Hardie, they moved to a one-roomed home near the Glasgow shipyard where David Hardie worked.

His father's wage was not enough to keep the family, especially when another son was born. At the age of eight Keir Hardie went out to work as an errand boy. When he was ten his wages of 3s 6d a week were all the family had to live on as his father was out of work. His mother and brother fell ill and Keir stayed up nearly all night to care for them. He was late for work next morning and his employer immediately sacked him and fined him a whole week's wages. Two weeks later Keir's brother died.

He moved to work in a shipyard where only a few weeks later a friend was killed. He moved again, this time to work in a pit at Hamilton. The ten-year-old boy sat in darkness from 6 a.m. to 5.30 p.m. opening and shutting a door which controlled the air supply. When he was twelve he was put in charge of a pit pony and was lucky to come out alive after a fall of rock underground.

Keir Hardie worked as a miner until he was 23. His brothers went down the pit with him and all shared the tiny home in Hamilton with their mother. The house had been built by the mining company but there was neither piped water nor a lavatory. These conditions made Keir Hardie angry but not because he was unlucky. He knew that life was just as hard for hundreds of thousands of young people in the 1860s. Yet this was at a time when Britain was the mightiest industrial nation in the world.

These figures show the value of the foreign trade of four leading countries in 1870.

	£ million
United Kingdom	547
France	227
Germany	212
United States	165

Yet of these countries Britain had the smallest population:

	million
United States	$38\frac{1}{2}$
Germany	41
France	36
United Kingdom	$31\frac{3}{4}$

A rich man's club? The House of Commons in 1860

The river Clyde in the 1870s

Britain was not rich because of her size. It was because she had more people who worked in the factories, on the railways and in the mines instead of on farms. Britain's industrial working class was the largest in the world.

But you would have seen no sign of this if you had looked around the House of Commons in the 1860s. On its benches sat lawyers, businessmen, landowners and others from the middle and upper classes. Nearly all belonged to one of the two great parties, the Liberals and the Conservatives. There were no working men. Nor was there a party to represent them. Some years earlier a group of people called Chartists had demanded that working men should have the right to vote. They had failed. Yet in the 1860s, some M.P.s were asking whether it was not time to give the vote to working men.

Votes for working men

One Sunday in July 1866 a long procession of working men walked through London streets towards Hyde Park. At its head was Robert Applegarth, the secretary of the Carpenters' Union, and other trade union leaders. They were the first to reach the Park and find that the police had locked the gates. They decided to march off and hold their meeting in Trafalgar Square. Yet many men behind grew angry and jostled and pushed until the rusty old Park railings gave way. A crowd burst in. Some held meetings of their own but others got into fights with the police.

There were many such demonstrations in 1866, all calling for a second Reform Act. The first Reform Act of 1832 had laid down that the right to vote went only to men who lived in town houses worth more than £10 a year. This was high enough to keep all but a very few working men from voting. No agricultural worker could.

In the 1860s many Liberals felt that it was time to give the vote to at least some working men. They pointed to the valuable work of trade union leaders like Robert Applegarth, who was always on the side of law and order. Others felt that, if there were no reform, there would be more riots like those in Hyde Park.

The Conservative leader Disraeli saw a chance to steal the Liberals' ideas and win support from the working men. So a second Reform Act was

Robert Applegarth

Benjamin Disraeli, a Conservative Prime Minister

passed in 1867 by the Conservatives. The great change this made was that working men in towns could vote in Parliamentary elections for the first time in British history.

It was the Liberals who made most use of the Reform Act. They saw that there would now be many constituencies (districts which send an M.P. to parliament) where working men would be in a majority. In some places the working men in towns could vote in vote for Liberal M.P.s. This was true in Birmingham where a great Liberal Lord Mayor, Joseph Chamberlain, won support for his party when he gave the city new streets and housing and its own gas and water supplies.

But in other places the new working

men voters could not be persuaded to vote for the Liberal candidates who were businessmen or lawyers. So in these constituencies the Liberal Party began to put up trade union leaders for election. If they won they supported the Liberal Party in the House of Commons. For this reason they were known as Liberal-Labour M.P.s or Lib-Labs.

In 1884 the Third Reform Act was passed. This gave working men in country districts the right to vote. Farm labourers were too few in each constituency to make any difference. The real importance of the Act was that the men who lived in the mining villages in the north of England, Scotland and the Welsh valleys could now vote.

Lib-Labs

Among the new M.P.s who came to the House of Commons after the election in 1874 were two Liberals, Thomas Burt and Alexander Macdonald. Both were miners, the first working men ever to be elected to the British Parliament. They were the first of the Lib-Labs. A third, Henry Broadhurst, was elected in 1881.

What sort of man became a Lib-Lab M.P.? All of them were leaders of unions either for miners or for skilled workers such as engineers. There were no unions for the poor unskilled workers at this time. Henry Broadhurst was secretary of the Parliamentary committee of the Trades Union Congress (or T.U.C.). The T.U.C. was an annual meeting of the trade union movement. It was set up in 1868 and its Parliamentary committee looked after its affairs between each annual meeting. One of its important jobs was to choose the men who would stand for Parliament as Lib-Labs.

With men like Broadhurst at the head of the T.U.C., the Liberal Party had little to fear from its working men M.P.s. All of them agreed with the Liberal Party view that it was not for the government to interfere in the living and working conditions of the British people. They believed that this was a matter for the unions to argue out with the employers. The job of the state was simply to act as an umpire. In Parliament the Lib-Labs pressed for laws which allowed the trade unions to bargain. But the idea of Parliament laying down hours of work or fixing wages horrified them just as much as the other Liberal M.P.s.

As union leaders the Lib-Labs set their face against going on strike unless everything else failed. This policy often led to quarrels with more fiery local

A colliery near Glasgow. The drawing was made after an underground explosion which killed many miners

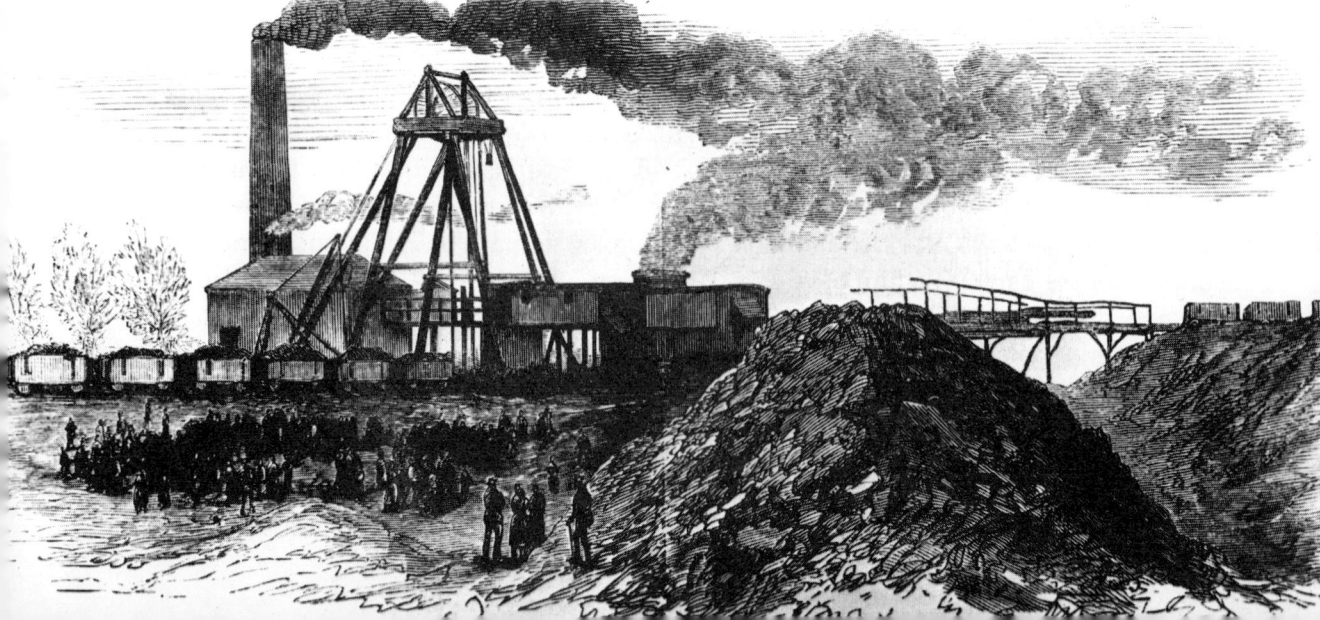

Two Lib-Lab M.P.s, Alexander MacDonald and Henry Broadhurst

trade unionists. One broke out between Alexander Macdonald, a Lib-Lab miners' leader, and Keir Hardie.

The year was 1879 and Keir Hardie had worked in the pit at Hamilton for thirteen years. His mother had taught him to read and he spent most of his spare time with books. This was one of the reasons why his fellow miners listened to him carefully when he spoke at their local union meetings. In 1879 the pit owners said they would have to cut the men's wages. Keir Hardie called on the men to stand up to the owners. They agreed to follow him in a strike if the pay was cut. The next day Keir Hardie was sacked from his job in the pit and was told that he and his family must leave their home,

which belonged to the mine company. Yet he stayed on in the district to help the men in a strike against lower wages. He and other leaders bought potatoes from local shopkeepers and promised to pay for them after the strike. For twelve weeks the miners stayed out and lived on the potatoes. The 'tattie strike' was successful because wages were not cut. Yet, when it was over, the only person who could raise the money to pay the shopkeepers was Alexander Macdonald who was both a Lib-Lab M.P. and chairman of the National Mineworkers Union. He had been against the strike and looked on Keir Hardie as a wild rebel. He refused to find the money for the potatoes unless Hardie left the district.

Keir Hardie

The Scottish Labour Party

Macdonald had his way and Keir Hardie left Lanarkshire. He went to the next county, Ayrshire. Here he became secretary of the Miners' Union. For twelve years he struggled to keep the union going. The miners lived in scattered villages and often Keir Hardie walked twelve or more miles across the moors to get from one meeting to the next. For four years the miners could not afford to pay him. Luckily his travelling meant he could earn £1 a week by sending reports of local news to a paper.

In 1887 he made use of this news-paper experience and started a small journal, *The Miner*. In it he began to campaign for a law to limit the miners' working day to eight hours. Hardie went to London to try to persuade M.P.s to back him. He came away disappointed with what he had seen of Parliament and above all with the Lib-Lab M.P.s. Even the miner M.P.s would not stand up for an eight-hour day. They followed the Liberal Party line that such matters were not the business of Parliament. Hardie wrote about them scornfully: 'What difference will it make to me that I have a working man representing me in Parliament, if he is a dumb dog who dare not bark and will follow the leader under any circumstance.'

He soon had a chance to show that he was true to his words. In 1888 the M.P. for Mid-Lanark resigned. Mid-Lanark was the district where Keir Hardie had led the 'tattie strike' and he decided to put himself up against the Liberal candidate. The Liberal Party asked him not to stand in return for a chance to fight a safe seat as a Lib-Lab in another election. They also promised him £300 a year when he became a Lib-Lab M.P. Hardie turned them down sharply: 'I do not want to be sent to Parliament by the money of rich men, nor to be kept by them. I want to be sent to Parliament by working men, to be paid by working men and kept by working men to speak for working men.'

He stood as an independent Labour candidate and was beaten heavily. But the election won its place in history. Only a few weeks after, Keir Hardie and his supporters set up the Scottish Labour Party to carry on the fight to elect independent working men to Parliament. They declared war on the Lib-Labs saying: 'The man who poses as a Liberal and yet refuses to support shorter working hours, an improve-ment in the homes of the people, the organisation of relief works for the unemployed...may call himself what he pleases...but he is an enemy.'

The Scottish Labour Party was the first in Britain to call itself Socialist. It called for 'social ownership' by all the people of the business which produced wealth for just a few. It demanded the nationalisation of land, mines and transport as well as heavy taxes on the rich, free education for all children and the abolition of the House of Lords. These policies were new and strange to most people except for a handful of supporters of small Socialist groups in London.

The last part of the message which Keir Hardie had printed and sent to the electors of Mid-Lanark

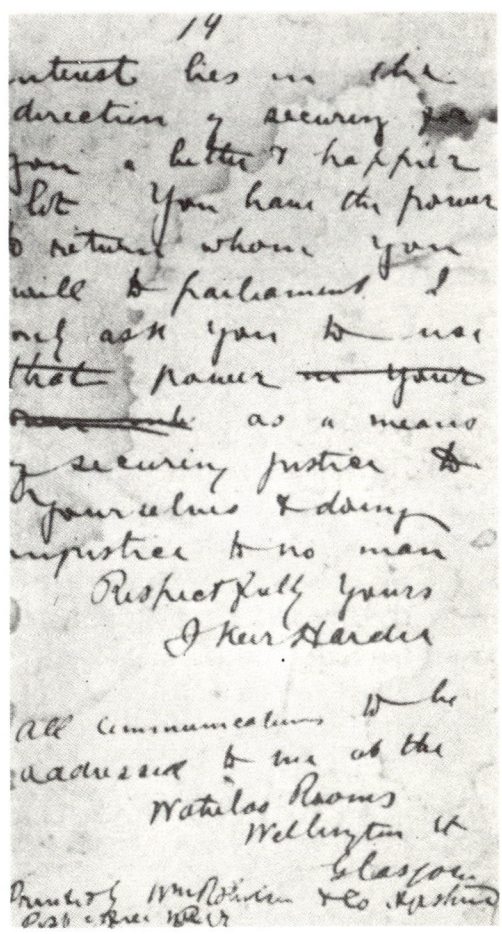

Marx and Engels

There are statues of Marx and Engels, the founders of Communism, in many Russian towns

Among this group of London Socialists was Friedrich Engels. Forty years earlier he had left his home in Germany to work in Manchester. The cotton trade of that great city lay behind England's growing wealth. Manchester businessmen were proud of the huge industrial centre which they had built up into the world's largest manufacturing town. Friedrich Engels, however, saw another side to Manchester life. It was a divided city:

'The upper classes enjoy healthy country air and live in luxurious and comfortable dwellings which are linked to the centre of Manchester by coaches which run every fifteen or thirty minutes. These plutocrats [members of a wealthy ruling class] can travel from their houses to their place of business in the centre of the town by the shortest routes, which run entirely through working class districts without ever realising how close they are to the misery and filth which lies on both sides of the road.'

He went on to describe some of these working class districts:

'In the houses one seldom sees a wooden or a stone floor, while the doors and windows are nearly always broken and badly fitting. And as for the dirt! Everywhere one sees heaps of refuse, garbage and filth.'

It was Engels's friend, Karl Marx, who had drawn a lesson for the future from these conditions. Marx taught that the new industry of the nineteenth century would lead to a class struggle between the working classes and their masters. These masters were Capitalists. That is, they were men with the funds or capital to start up factories, mines and so on. An industrial country like England was a Capitalist state where the government, Parliament, the law all worked in the interests of the men who owned the factories and businesses. While they had this power said Marx nothing would be done to improve the wretchedness of working-class life as Engels had described it. He believed that better times would come only when the working classes became powerful enough to take industry away from the Capitalists.

Karl Marx had to live in England because he was looked on as a dangerous revolutionary in his own land of Germany. From London his ideas spread. Marxists were behind many of the trade union and Socialist movements which sprang up in the countries of Europe and in Russia. Yet it was not until the 1880s, just before Marx died, that the first English Marxist organisation was founded.

Engels wrote his description of Manchester in 1844. These photographs show rich and poor families fifty years later

Stockbroker and poet

The first English Marxist was Henry Hyndman. He did not fit most people's idea of a Socialist for he was a stockbroker and always dressed in a smart frock coat with a black top hat. It was often said that he was interested in politics mostly because it brought him to people's notice. H. M. Hyndman wrote two books which put forward Marx's ideas into English for the first time. Marx wasn't very pleased for, at first, Hyndman did not admit that the ideas were not his own.

In 1884, the year after Karl Marx died, Hyndman started the Social Democratic Federation (S.D.F.). Like the Scottish Labour Party it put forward Socialist policies. Most important was the 'socialisation of the means of production, distribution and exchange'. This meant taking industry and business away from their Capitalist owners and handing them over to the whole people. There were different ways of doing this: you could nationalise industries and have them run by the government; you could municipalise them and let local councils take charge; you could let the workers run their own factories. Socialists differed about which was the best way but until recently all agreed that you must have some form of socialisation to take wealth and power

A special number of the S.D.F. paper 'Justice'

The manifesto of the Socialist League

away from the Capitalists.

It was not long before S.D.F. members began to complain that Hyndman would not let them take part in discussions freely. Many left the S.D.F. after one year and set up the Socialist League. Its leader was William Morris, a poet and designer. Morris had always hated the misery and ugliness of life in the age of machines and factories. 'We should be masters of our machines and not their slaves as we are now', he once said. In his early- and middle-age he had carried on the struggle against ugliness by designing wallpapers, tapestries and beautiful books. When he was nearly 50 he came to believe that money-making was the cause of the evils. Morris became a Socialist. He wrote that it was because a few men wanted to make profits that others were crowded into cramped houses, that the air was filled with smoke and beautiful rivers turned into filthy sewers.

William Morris

Part of a page from a book of Chaucer's poetry designed by William Morris

In *News from Nowhere* Morris imagined a time after the misery of working men's lives had led to revolution. After winning their freedom the workers built a happier society. People returned from city slums to the villages. They left factories for small pleasant workshops. Men no longer cared for making huge quantities of goods to sell, so the filthy dock areas once again became pleasant ports. You could catch salmon in the Thames as it was no longer polluted with London's dirt.

Neither Hyndman nor Morris was a good political leader. But some of the men who joined the S.D.F. and the Socialist League were amongst the most important Socialists of the next twenty years.

Socialists at work

Inside a gas-works

One of the first working men to join the S.D.F. was Will Thorne. He had never been to school and had worked from early childhood. For many years he was a labourer in gasworks up and down the country. Every town had its gas-works where men toiled for twelve-hour shifts. Half-choked by fumes they raked red-hot cinders from the furnaces or filled them with buckets of coke pulled along wires. Sometimes the wires broke and killed a worker below.

In March 1889 Will Thorne called an outdoor meeting of gasworkers in London. He asked them to start a union and fight for an eight hour day. There and then 800 men threw a shilling membership fee into a pail. Three months later the number had risen to 20,000 and the union had 66 branches.

Six months later they demanded an eight-hour day. The owners gave it immediately for they feared a public outcry if the terrible conditions in their gasworks became known.

Ben Tillett was another member of the S.D.F. who was an uneducated labourer. He worked in the London docks. Just after the gasworkers had won their victory, a group of dockers asked for sixpence instead of fivepence an hour for a very dirty job. The owners refused so the men struck. Tillett immediately came along to help and called in two friends he had made in S.D.F., John Burns and Tom Mann.

The three Socialists turned this small strike of men working on one ship into stoppage of work in all of London's docks. Each day John Burns led a great procession of dockers through London. He gave reporters details of the wretched lives of the dockers' families. Money began to pour in from a shocked public. The greatest sum of all came from Australia where private citizens, trade unions and football clubs collected altogether £30,000. It was Tom Mann's job to give this to the strikers. Eventually the dock owners agreed to talk to the men and said they would pay them sixpence an hour.

Victory meant far more than the dockers' tanner; it was the start of new unionism. The dockers and gasworkers had founded the first 'general' unions for unskilled workers. Their success

At a table, from right to left, Tom Mann, Ben Tillett, John Burns issue food tickets for striking dockers

Will Thorne

seemed to show that tough strike action gave better results than the bargaining which the older trade union leaders believed in. The older trade unions leaders were Liberals. The new unions were led by Socialists. Which were more fitted to stand up for the rights of England's working men? Every year when the T.U.C. met this question was argued. Keir Hardie called for the trade unions to break all connections with the Liberals. He was supported by Tom Mann, Ben Tillett and Will Thorne who argued that Lib-Lab leaders like Henry Broadhurst should stand down and that independent working men should be put up for Parliament. The idea of Socialism was gaining strength. Its next great step forward came in Yorkshire in 1891.

Workers in Yorkshire

Life was grim in the 1880s for the workers of Leeds, Bradford and the surrounding districts. Trade had begun to fall off as more and more countries began to manufacture their own textiles. To keep in business the factory owners cut their workers' wages. They employed a great number of women and children even though this was against the law.

Most of the workers were unskilled and did not have much of a will to fight low wages or the shocking housing conditions. They got no support from the leaders of the Trade unions in Leeds and Bradford for these were all men from the unions of skilled workers. So, just as the miners in Scotland turned to Keir Hardie and the dockers to John Burns, the unskilled workers of Yorkshire turned to local Socialists. A small band of young men in their twenties including Tom Maguire and Fred Jowett had learned their Socialism in the same way as Ben Tillett and Tom Mann. They had first joined a branch of the S.D.F. and then moved into William Morris's Socialist League.

Soon they were busy helping the unskilled workers. An 800-strong union of bricklayers' labourers grew up and won a strike for an extra halfpenny an hour. Tom Maguire then helped the tailoresses in Leeds to form a union. He wrote them a song:

Every worker in every trade
In Britain and everywhere
Whether he labour by needle or spade
Shall gather in his rightful share.

A nineteenth century cartoon: 'The cheap tailor and his workmen'

Fred Jowett

Ben Tillett

A gasworkers' union was started and Will Thorne came to help get it organised.

Then followed the great strike at Manningham Mills in Bradford which lasted from December 1890 to April 1891. Nearly 5,000 workers took part in a struggle to prevent their wages being cut. Although Ben Tillett came up to help the strike was a miserable failure.

The Socialists in Yorkshire found that they had not got the public sympathy that the dockers had in London. The reason was that nearly every important position in the woollen district was held by a Liberal. The men on the town councils and the education boards, and most of the local M.P.s'

were Liberals. The local trade union leaders were supporters of the Liberal Party and Lib-Lab policies. The Socialists decided to hit hard at local Liberals at elections. So in May 1891, just one month after the Manningham Mills Strike, the Bradford Independent Labour Party was formed. In 1892 there was a Parliamentary election in Bradford West. The Bradford I.L.P. asked Ben Tillett to stand. He lost to the Liberals but only by 600 votes.

Now there were two Socialist parties the Scottish Labour Party and the Bradford Independent Labour Party. Both were ready to put forward Socialist candidates and have nothing more to do with the Lib-Labs.

M.P. for the unemployed

Ben Tillett's defeat in Bradford was a disappointment. It was followed by one great triumph in the 1892 general election. Hardie was asked to stand as an independent Labour candidate for the London district of South West Ham, the home of many dockers who had taken part in the great strike four years before. Day after day Hardie went down to the dock gates to make his election speeches. In one he said:

'It is not my fight, men, it is yours. It is you who will lose or win. If you return me to the House of Commons I will fight for you. I have seen men waiting to work at the dock gate, standing there as if they were so many heads of cattle. 'One man, one vote', as John Burns says is good but 'One man, one job and a job for every man is better'.

After the votes were counted these figures were announced:

Keir Hardie   5,268
Major G. E. Barnes   4,036

A poster for the South West Ham election

VOTE FOR

Home Rule.

Democratic Government.

Justice to Labour

No Monopoly.

No Landlordism

Temperance Reform.

Healthy Homes.

Fair Rents.

Eight-Hour Day.

Work for the Unemployed.

KEIR HARDIE.

Printed and Published by F W Scr se & Co. [L S C], 151, Barking Road, Canning Town, London, E.

Miners' families wait at the pit-head for news after the Welsh colliery disaster

Keir Hardie was Member of Parliament for South West Ham and the first Labour M.P. in Britain's history.

His docker friends decided that he must go to Parliament in style. They hired a wagonette and a crowd squeezed in beside him. One played a cornet noisily. It was certainly a most unusual entrance into Parliament. Keir Hardie's appearance horrified the other M.P.s. The Lib-Labs—there were twelve in parliament at the time—all had the decency to turn up in dark suits and wearing bowlers. Hardie wore 'an old deerstalker cap and check suit you could have played draughts on'.

But this was not the important difference between Hardie and the Lib-Labs. They were members of the Liberal Party which had won the election. Hardie would not sit with the government. He sat on the opposition side of the House of Commons. From there he kept up a lonely struggle to draw attention to the problems of working men and particularly the unemployed. Time and again he criticised the government for taking no action over unemployment. He soon became known by many as 'member for the unemployed'.

He could not always hide his hatred for the Liberals and Conservatives. In June 1894 the Duke and Duchess of York had a son. The House of Commons met to send a message of congratulation. On the same day there was a terrible mining disaster in south Wales in which 250 men had been killed. Nothing was said about this in the House of Commons so Hardie got up to speak against sending the message to the Royal Family when Parliament would not send one to the

'relatives of those who are lying stiff and stark in a Welsh valley.'

He had to stand alone before a hail of cat-calls and jeers. As the reporter for the *West Ham Herald* wrote:

'They howled and screamed but he stood his ground.'

The I.L.P.

After the 1892 victory Keir Hardie was a name known to every working man in Britain. His victory at West Ham gave heart to the trade unionists and Socialists who believed that the time had come for a separate party for working men.

That autumn they held a meeting in Glasgow with Keir Hardie as chairman. It was agreed to join the different Socialist groups together into a national party. They decided to call a conference to start the new party at Bradford, a place where the Socialists had been very active.

The conference was held in January 1893. Speeches were made like this one by a journalist Socialist, Robert Blatchford:

> 'I regard Liberals and Tories as enemies of the people. When I say a man is my enemy I mean I hate him and will fight him to the death. I cannot understand why I should take that man's hand. I would consider it a stain on the Labour Party to have any dealings with the Liberals. I would as soon have dealings with the devil.'

After more discussion those at the conference decided to call themselves the Independent Labour Party (or I.L.P.) to make it clear that they aimed to build up an organisation which had no connection with the Liberals.

The greatest problem was money. Trade unions were the only working

Keir Hardie's I.L.P. membership card

class groups with much money. Most of them refused to have anything to do with the I.L.P. So when the next election came in 1895 it was a great disappointment. The I.L.P. did manage to put up candidates for 28 of the 630 seats in Parliament. Yet not one was elected. Even Keir Hardie lost his seat at West Ham. There was no I.L.P. man in parliament until 1900.

But the years were not wasted. Hardie went on campaigning with just as much energy as before. All the time he wrote weekly articles for his news-paper *The Labour Leader*. Very often these were written late at night in cold hotel rooms miles away from home; perhaps after an evening spent making an outdoor speech in the pouring rain.

Yet Keir Hardie was not alone. The I.L.P. collected many keen supporters, often young men and women who gave all their energy to fighting for the

new cause. J. Bruce Glasier gave up
his job to help with *The Labour Leader*
and wrote poetry which expressed the
Socialist belief that a new age was just
around the corner:

> 'O, the world is overburdened
> With the idle and the rich!
> They bask up in the sunshine
> While we plod in the ditch;
> But, zounds! we'll put some mettle
> In their fingers and their thumbs,
> For we'll turn things upside down,
>   my lads,
> When the Revolution comes.'

J. Bruce Glasier

*A cartoonist forecast disaster when Keir Hardie cut off Labour's connection with the
Liberal Party*

'The Clarion'

'I walked with difficulty, with the aid of a stick, every step a deliberate effort, carrying my bag in the other hand, I made all the journeys alone. I spoke in practically every large town in Great Britain, in most of them very often, and in hundreds of smaller towns and villages. I often had to travel long distances between meetings, and frequently was unable to get food between breakfast time and evening.'

This is how Philip Snowden, a weaver's son who was crippled in early life, spent the ten years from 1896 to 1906. Like most of his fellows he saw the cause as almost a religious one, a struggle to make the right and good win over evil. His speeches were

Philip Snowden

famous for the way they ended with what one friend called 'a bit of Come to Jesus'.

The work of these men and women who spoke at meetings inside and out brought the I.L.P. to the notice of hundreds and thousands of Englishmen. Others helped the cause by their work on local councils. One great I.L.P. pioneer was Margaret Macmillan who fought for nursery schools where the wretchedly poor infants of Bradford could get decent care during the day. But perhaps the most important supporter of the I.L.P. in his day was Robert Blatchford.

Early in life he had been a brush-maker and then a soldier. Then he became a journalist on the *Sunday Chronicle* earning £1,000 a year. In 1890 he read a pamphlet written by H. M. Hyndman and William Morris. This made him a Socialist. He used his weekly article to expose conditions in Manchester slums, signing them with the name Nunquam. The Chronicle's owner called him in. 'No Socialism in my paper, he said. Then no 'Nunquam,'' said Blatchford and walked out with his brother and two journalist friends. Together they borrowed £500 to start a Socialist newspaper, *The Clarion*. After a long search they found a printer and and someone who would give them the paper.

The first issue was a mess because the paper was poor quality. Still, nearly

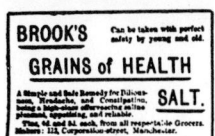

The front page of 'The Clarion'

40,000 people bought it. For the next ten years *The Clarion* sold a large number like this. It did more than anything else to turn people to Socialism. Blatchford built up a wide organisation to sell his paper and his ideas. Clarion clubs were started for political discussion. Young men and women joined Clarion cycling clubs which spent weekends in the country enjoying themselves, talking politics, putting up posters and selling *The Clarion*. Clarion horse-drawn vans went around advertising the paper with speakers who stopped to talk when ever they could draw a crowd.

Robert Blatchford lived to be ninety. He once said 'I am an average Briton,' and he certainly knew how to write for average Britons. His most famous articles in *The Clarion* were a series called 'Merrie England' written to Mr John Smith—or all the common people of England. When they were put together in a book ¾ million copies were read in one year.

Margaret Macmillan

Dear Mr Smith

Robert Blatchford

Dear Mr Smith,

I am sorry to hear that you look upon Socialism as a vile and senseless thing, and upon Socialists as wicked or foolish men.

Nevertheless, as you have good metal in you and, are very numerous, I mean to argue the point with you.

Of every thousand persons who die in Merrie England over nine hundred die without leaving any property at all. About eight millions of people exist always on the borders of destitution. About twenty millions are poor.

Political orators and newspaper editors are very fond of talking to you about 'your country'. Now, Mr Smith, it is a hard practical fact that you have not got any country. The British Islands do not belong to the British people; they belong to a few thousands— certainly not half a million—of rich men.

For you know very well that it is true of nearly all our working men that they cannot work when they choose to work, but must first find a rich man—a Capitalist—who is willing to employ them.

This is because the Capitalists own the land and the tools. What can the ploughman do without the land and the plough; or the collier without the pit and the machinery; or the weaver without the loom and the factory?

Therefore the land, the factories, the railways, ships and machinery do not belong to the people, but to a few rich men.

Therefore the land, the factories, railways, ships and machinery are not used for the general good of the people, but are used to make wealth for the few rich men who own them.

Socialists say that this arrangement is unjust and unwise, that it entails waste as well as misery, and that it would be better for all, even for the rich, that the land and other instruments of production should become the property of the state, just as the post-office and the telegraphs have become the property of the State.

Socialists point out that if all the industries of the nation were put under state control, all the profit which now goes into the hands of a few idle men, would go into the coffers of the state—which means that the people would enjoy the benefits of all the wealth they create.

This, then, is the basis of Socialism, that England should be owned by the English, instead of being owned by a few rich idlers, and mismanaged by them for the benefit of themselves.

Robert Blatchford.

'Therefore the factories do no belong to the people but to a few rich men'

The Fabians

Beatrice and Sidney Webb

A Fabian Society membership card

From the diary of a well-to-do woman describing a fortnight with her fiancé in the north of England:

'16 October 1891 Yesterday evening we spent at a public-house in Newcastle interviewing plumbers and today we have been hard at work on rules and reports.'

A year later Beatrice Potter and Sidney Webb married and began what she called 'our partnership'. By this time Sidney Webb had given up his job in the Civil Service and soon they published the first of the many books which came out of their partnership.

Beatrice and Sidney Webb were two of the best-known members of the Fabian Society. This had started in 1884 among a group of middle-class Londoners. Its members were all Socialists who believed that they should work for gradual improvements in British life. The name Fabian was taken from the Roman general Fabius, who had tried to wear down his country's great enemy, Hannibal, by avoiding open battles which he hadn't the strength to win.

Beatrice Webb said their greatest task was to make 'thinking people Socialist'. This would only be done by presenting them with facts, about industry, government, the lives of the poor; facts which often took the Fabians months or even years to collect. With these facts they hoped to persuade men in Parliament or local government that changes were necessary. They were particularly interested in 'gas and water Socialism'. By this they meant improvements in local supplies of not only gas and water but of such things as education and welfare services.

The Webbs were probably the best Fabians at producing facts. Another famous Fabian was the play writer George Bernard Shaw. He put over Fabian ideas in a way which was difficult to forget. In one pamphlet he wrote:

'The established government has no more right to call itself the state than the smoke of London has to call itself the weather.'

In another he discussed the difficult problem of why a luxury item cost so much more than the cost of the materials and wages which were needed to make it. He began by putting the problem in these words: 'A New York Lady, for instance,... orders and elegant rosewood and silver coffin, upholstered in pink satin, for her dead dog. It is made; and meanwhile a live child is prowling barefooted and hunger-stunted in the frozen gutter outside.'

The Fabians were always few in numbers but they played an important part in making Socialist ideas well-known and in putting forward Socialist plans which would actually work.

George Bernard Shaw

'... a live child is prowling'.
A photograph taken in 1895

The Labour Representation Committee

The London engineers struck for an eight hour day. Here they put their case at an outdoor meeting

In 1897 some London engineers went on strike. Engineering employers throughout the country closed their works to trade union engineers. They were arranging a lockout to help the London employers defeat the engineers trade union.

Keir Hardie wrote about the lockout: 'For seven long weary months the men fought grimly. Gaunt poverty, like a hungry wolf, was the occupant of tens of thousands of homes.' He went on to complain about the Lib-Labs who had ignored the way the employers had driven men from work. 'The engineers have probably noticed that these 'working men who go to Parliament by the grace of the Liberal Whip are not so very different from the other men who are there.'

In the end the engineers had to go back to work defeated. This was just one of the many lockouts of the 1890s which alarmed trade union leaders who found that the employers had a strong weapon against them. Many more trade union leaders were now ready to listen to Socialists who argued that there must be a separate Labour Party to protect the interests of labour.

These were the men behind a proposal which was brought forward at the 1899 T.U.C. meeting. There it was agreed that the T.U.C. call a meeting of trade unions, co-operative societies and Socialist groups to work out ways of 'securing an increased number of Labour members in the next Parliament'.

The meeting was held in London in January 1900. There were 116 men from 65 trade unions, a few representatives from the S.D.F. and the Fabian Society as well as Keir Hardie and 6 other members of the I.L.P. They quickly agreed to set up a Labour Representation Committee to work for the election of a separate group of Labour M.P.s in the House of Commons.

Before the meeting closed they had to make some important decisions. One was whether the new group should work only to get working men into Parliament or whether any one who was sympathetic to the problems of the working men should be able to stand for the new organisation. Some unionists were in favour of sending only working men. Others disagreed. One said:
'I am getting tired of working-class boots, working-class brains, working-class houses and working-class margarine. I believe the time has come when we should not be prisoners to class prejudice.'

Most people agreed with this and the way was open for men and women like those in the Fabian Society to become members of the new Labour organisation.

James Ramsay MacDonald on his 21st birthday

The Labour Party

The 29 Labour M.P.s on the terrace of the House of Commons in 1906

Only a few months after the L.R.C. was set up it had to be ready to fight a general election. Short of funds and with only a handful of supporters, all it could do was to put up fifteen candidates for Parliament. Only two were elected. One was Keir Hardie. This time he became M.P. for the Welsh town of Merthyr Tydfil. The other Labour M.P. soon began to move towards the Liberals so Keir Hardie was once again alone in the House of Commons.

But outside Parliament the L.R.C.

was increasing its strength. Its Scottish secretary, Ramsay MacDonald, worked hard to build up support among the trade unions, for their money would be needed to fight the next election. He was helped by the Taff Vale decision. The courts backed the Taff Vale company when it sued the railwaymen's union for £23,000 to make up for the business it had lost during a strike. All unions were now in danger unless they could get the law changed so many more became willing to support the L.R.C. with funds. The

Liberals saw that they would have tough fights against the L.R.C. in working-class constituencies. So they secretly agreed with Ramsay MacDonald that Liberals would not stand in some of these districts if the L.R.C. would not fight in some others.

Ramsay MacDonald's work had its reward in the 1906 election. 29 Labour M.P.s were elected. Nearly $\frac{1}{3}$ million people had voted Labour. There were enough M.P.s to turn the L.R.C. into a party. The first chairman of the new Labour Party was Keir Hardie. In the party with him was Ramsay MacDonald who later became Britain's first Labour Prime Minister and three other M.P.s who were to be Cabinet ministers.

Keir Hardie did not live to see these great triumphs. He died in 1916 worn out by his struggles for Socialism. In his last years he often thought that his fellow M.P.s were more concerned with making their party strong than with building a better world. He was one of a handful who believed that Britain should not take part in World War One. This struggle, he argued, was nothing to do with the real battle for a happier life.

This was the cause for which he had struggled since those early days as a miner in Hamilton. When he died one Labour M.P. wrote: 'On the day that the common people enter into the Promised Land, no name deserves to be more affectionately and gratefully remembered than Keir Hardie.'

Keir Hardie, the first chairman of the Labour Party

To write

1 Make up a time-line showing the most important events in the life of Keir Hardie.
2 Write two or three sentences saying why each of the following were important: *The Miner, The Clarion, News from Nowhere*.
3 How did each of the following strikes play a part in the growth of Socialism: the 'tattie strike', the dock strike, the Manningham Mills strike?
4 What part did the following groups of people play in the development of the Labour Movement: Robert Applegarth, Henry Broadhurst and Alexander MacDonald; William Morris, Beatrice Webb and George Bernard Shaw; Will Thorne, Ben Tillett and Tom Maguire?
5 Which important events in the rise of the Labour Party happened in each of the years: 1884, 1889, 1891, 1892, 1900, 1906?
6 Write two or three sentences about each of: the Scottish Labour Party, the S.D.F., the I.L.P. and the L.R.C.

For discussion

1 Socialist ideas or bad living conditions? Which most helped the growth of the Labour Party?
2 Do you agree with William Morris that *We should be masters of our machines and not their slaves?*
3 Are there problems in Britain today which will not be solved without a new political party?
4 What makes a good M.P.? Should he or she come from the same class or work in the same trade as his or her electors?
5 How much of what Robert Blatchford wrote to Mr Smith is true of Britain today?

To find out

1 In which years has Britain been governed by the Labour Party in the twentieth century?
2 What changes in British life were made during the Attlee government?
3 How many people voted for the Labour Party in the last general election? How many seats in Parliament did it win?
4 Find out as much as you can about the life of Robert Owen, one of the first English Socialists.
5 This book mentions the Second and Third Reform Acts. Read about the First Reform Act (1832) and find out when women were given the vote in the twentieth century.
6 Read the following books in this folder: *The Chartists, Education for the People, The Health of the People*.

After reading all the books in the set

1 Write a comparison between social life in Britain between 1870 and 1914 and between 1800 and 1830.
2 Make a list of the social problems that followed from the industrialisation of Britain. Show what was done, up to 1914, to tackle each one and which person or group of people was involved in the improvement.
3 Make a chart gathering together all the information that you can find in these five books about the lives of children.
4 England in the nineteenth century has often been described as a land of two nations— the rich and the poor. Find examples from each book which show this.